READ MARK LEARN

D1323941

READ MARK LEARN

John Blanchard

 EVANGELICAL PRESS

EVANGELICAL PRESS
12 Wooler Street, Darlington, Co. Durham, DL1 1RQ, England.

© Evangelical Press 1987
First published 1966
Second edition 1966
Third edition 1976
Fourth edition 1979
Seventeenth impression 1988

ISBN 0 85234 234 9

All Scripture references are from the *New International Version*,
Hodder & Stoughton, 1984.

Typeset by Berea Press, Glasgow.
Printed in Great Britain by Cox & Wyman, Reading.

Introduction

Welcome into the Christian family! In saying that, I am assuming that you have just recently become a Christian, and that you have bought, or been given, this booklet to help you to read and understand the Bible. I do hope it will!

The Bible has several ways of describing a Christian. It says that that person has been 'saved', or 'converted', or 'born again', and this last phrase tells a new Christian the marvellous truth that he or she now belongs to God's family. The apostle John puts it like this: 'To all who received him [the Lord Jesus Christ], to those who believed in his name, he gave the right to become children of God' (John 1:12).

When he died on the cross Jesus paid the penalty for your sin, and when he rose again from the dead he conquered both sin and death on your behalf. By receiving the Lord Jesus Christ, you have not just made a new start in life, you have received a new life to start with! As a child of God you can know that you have been set free from the guilt of sin, and that you can claim his power to overcome temptation, to control your thoughts, words and actions, and to live a life that is pleasing to him.

From now on you can trust God's promises in a *personal* way, promises like the one in John 10:28 where Jesus says, 'I give them eternal life, and they shall never perish.' What a wonderful promise that is! It means that you can be sure of remaining a child of God *for ever*, and that *nothing* can ever cut you off from him! As John says, 'Whoever believes in the Son has eternal life' (John 3:36).

But a new-born baby needs to grow! Birth is only the beginning of life, and the 'new birth' is only the beginning of spiritual life. How can you grow spiritually? I hope to show you that as we go through this little book together, but let me give you two vital pieces of advice before we start.

1. Make sure that you pray! Prayer is not just asking God for things. It is a way that God has provided for you to keep in daily touch with him. In prayer, you will be able to thank him for his goodness, seek his guidance and power, and pray for his blessing on your life and on the lives of others.

2. Read your Bible regularly. Writing to Christians who had not long been converted, the apostle Peter urged them: 'Like newborn babies, crave pure spiritual milk, so that by it you may grow up in your salvation, now that you have tasted that the Lord is good' (1 Peter 2:2-3).

Just as a physical baby grows by regularly drinking pure milk, so God's children find the Bible to be his perfect way of providing spiritual food for them.

But as a new Christian you are probably asking, 'Where should I start?' That is where *Read, Mark, Learn* comes in!

In the New Testament there are four 'Gospels', each telling the story of Christ's life here on earth. The shortest, and probably the first to be written, is the one by Mark. What I have done in this booklet is to divide Mark's Gospel into forty-five daily readings, and then to write a page of notes on each passage. By following these readings and notes you can study the life of Christ in just over six weeks, and in doing so learn a great deal about the Christian life.

I suggest that you use the booklet in this way:

1. As you come to the Bible each day, take time to pray that God will help you to understand what you are about to read.

2. Read slowly and carefully the passage indicated at the top of the page (for example, on the first day read Mark 1, verses 1-11).

3. Read the notes, looking back to the passage in Mark whenever a particular verse is quoted, and looking up every other Bible reference as it is mentioned.

4. Look up the text quoted at the foot of the page, and think about how it fits in with the day's reading.

5. Keep a notebook handy and jot down anything you think is especially helpful.

6. Pray that God will help you to live out the implications of whatever particular truths he has shown you from his Word.

Now you will want to begin your first reading. May God richly bless you in these coming days, and help you to 'grow in the grace and knowledge of our Lord and Saviour Jesus Christ' (2 Peter 3:18).

Footnote:

In preparing this edition of *Read, Mark, Learn* I have used the *New International Version* of the Bible. It has a very good claim to being the best English translation now available and I would strongly urge you to obtain a copy, at least for use with these notes.

Forgiven!

You have just begun the Christian life and this is the beginning of your daily times of regular Bible reading as a Christian. Surely there could be no better words to start with than these: 'The beginning of the gospel . . .' (v.1). The word 'gospel' means 'good news' and these eleven verses tell us at least two things about it.

It was preached by John. What a wonderful gospel it was – and still is! 'The forgiveness of sins' (v.4): when God forgives a person's sins it means that they are wiped out and done away with! See the promise God made in Jeremiah 31:34. But notice that *before* a person can be forgiven there has to be 'repentance' (v.4). To repent is to change one's mind about a thing, leading to a change of attitude and behaviour. In the case of sin it means to turn one's back on it completely. Notice how Jesus linked repentance and the gospel in verse 15 (which comes in tomorrow's reading). Are you sure that you have obeyed his command? If so, you can certainly claim God's promise.

It was provided by Jesus. The best news the world has ever heard is 'the gospel about Jesus Christ, the Son of God' (v.1). John knew that he was preparing the way for someone 'more powerful than I' (v.7). John was the messenger; Jesus was the message! Jesus allowed himself to be baptized by John, not because he had any sin of his own of which he needed to repent (read carefully what is said in Hebrews 4:15), but to identify himself with sinful men. The Son of God left the glory of heaven to be identified with us in his birth, his baptism, his life and, above all, in his death, for as Peter reminds us, 'He himself bore our sins in his body on the tree' (1 Peter 2:24). Jesus was more than an example; he took your place in order to undergo the death penalty due because of your sin. *He* died so that *you* might be forgiven! Take time now to rejoice in that wonderful fact!

'In Christ God forgave you' (Ephesians 4:32).

Three great possessions

This passage includes the calling of the first disciples and a remarkable incident at Capernaum, but let us concentrate on just one verse and notice three great possessions which are now yours as a Christian.

In verse 17 you will first of all find *a person to follow.* Jesus found Simon (Peter) and his brother Andrew by the lakeside and commanded them: 'Come, follow me.' Immediately they turned their backs on everything else and followed him – and were never the same again! Now that he has called you to himself, be determined to follow Jesus, and to make him your pattern, your standard and your guide in every detail of your life.

Notice that the verse also speaks of *a power to fashion.* Jesus went on: '. . . and I will make you . . .' What power Jesus has! Power to create (John 1:3); power to cure (Matthew 8:3); power to control (Luke 8:24); but above all, power to change men's lives. Because Jesus now lives within you by his Holy Spirit, this power is now yours and is sufficient to deal with all your problems. The Bible says, 'It is God who works in you to will and to act according to his good purpose' (Philippians 2:13).

Notice at the end of the verse there is *a purpose to fulfil.* 'Fishers of men'. It is a marvellous thing to know that God has a pattern and a purpose for your life, and you can be sure that you will gradually see it working out as you follow him. Whatever that purpose may be, there is no doubt that it includes being a 'fisher of men'. Do not be ashamed of your Saviour, but begin now to pray that he will use you to draw others to him. See that you commend the Lord Jesus to others, not only by what you say, but by how you live. Matthew 5:16 puts it perfectly!

'Let us fix our eyes on Jesus, the author and perfecter of our faith' (Hebrews 12:2).

What a Saviour!

Today's reading covers four separate incidents, but if you look at them together, you will see that they illustrate two great truths about the Lord Jesus Christ.

His deep concern. What a variety of problems we find in this passage! Peter's mother-in-law was ill in bed, many of the neighbours had sickness of one kind or another, and a man found to his dismay that he had contracted the dread disease of leprosy – yet Jesus was concerned about them all! As he is 'the same yesterday and today and for ever' (Hebrews 13:8), you can be sure that he is concerned about every detail of *your* life. Nothing is so large that it leaves God incapable, and nothing is so small that it leaves him unconcerned. By the way, notice in verse 35 that Jesus began the day with prayer! Whatever it costs, arrange your day so that you can begin it by asking God to guide and bless you throughout the day's activities. If you want an example from the Old Testament, see what David wrote in Psalm 5:3!

His divine compassion. Compassion is much more than concern. It is love in action. Notice some of the things Jesus did. In verse 31 he went to Peter's mother-in-law and 'helped her up'; in verse 34 'he healed many'; in verse 41 he told the leper: 'Be clean!' Here is God's love in action, meeting people at the point of their individual need. As a young Christian, you may sense a special need to be 'helped up' from things that have spoilt your life so far; you will want to be 'healed' of the wounds and scars of past sin; and you will certainly need to be kept 'clean' day by day. As you recognize these needs, learn to realize that in the Lord Jesus Christ you have a Saviour who is wonderfully able to do all of these things!

'Cast all your anxiety on him, because he cares for you' (1 Peter 5:7).

Faith works!

These verses, which describe another incident at Capernaum, tell us several important things about 'faith', one of the most important words in the Bible. To have faith in a person means to trust or rely on that person.

Notice, however, that the story begins with **difficulties**. A man was paralysed (v.3). Only Jesus could cure him, but there was such a crowd of people that it seemed impossible to get near him. You may find yourself in that position at times, wondering just how you can bring a friend to Christ, or how some other problem can be solved.

But notice that some people had **determination.** Try to picture the extraordinary scene described in verse 4! As they could not get into the house through the door the four people concerned went up on to the flat roof and opened up the tiling (see Luke 5:19) to lower their friend through. So great was their love for the sick man and their faith in the power of Jesus to heal him that they would not take 'No' for an answer! They were prepared to go to any lengths to bring their problem to Christ and to ask him to deal with it. What an example to you as a Christian!

The marvellous result of all this was **deliverance.** It was 'when Jesus saw their faith' (v. 5) that he delivered the man, firstly of his sin (v. 5) and then of his sickness (vv. 11-12). The scribes were quite right to say that only God could forgive sin (v. 7) – but what they did not realize was that Jesus was God! (John 10:30 is one of the verses that tell us this.) You will soon find that the Christian life has many difficulties, and to some of them there may seem to be no answer. When this is the case, make sure nothing stops you taking them to Christ and trusting him to act in response to your faithful prayer.

'According to your faith will it be done to you' (Matthew 9:29).

Pressing on

Today's reading contains quite a mixture of incidents, but you can pick out several important points as you press on in these first days as a Christian.

Obedience. As soon as Jesus called him, Levi 'got up and followed him' (v.14). He could never have guessed what lay ahead, but he was prepared to trust Jesus for every step of life's journey, whatever the cost. We know that Levi took his gift of writing (he was a tax-collector) and consecrated it to the Lord's service, eventually writing the first book in the New Testament. You, too, have special gifts and abilities (see Ephesians 4:7). Make sure that they are available for use in God's service.

Opposition. The scribes and Pharisees criticized Jesus for mixing with people they classed as undesirables (v. 16). His answer was that he had not come to call those who felt that they were already good enough (v. 17). Then his disciples were criticized for not fasting (v. 18). Jesus answered that for his disciples to be mournful while he was with them was as unthinkable as for special guests to be miserable at a wedding (v. 19). The Christian life is meant to be a life of joy. (Look up Romans 14:17 and Philippians 4:4.)

Observance. Verses 23-28 deal with Sunday observance. There were many traditional Jewish laws about the Sabbath, some of them quite ridiculous. For instance, some Pharisees even taught that it was sinful to pluck a single ear of corn on that day! Jesus cut across all these regulations by saying, 'The Sabbath was made for man . . .' (v. 27); but note what he added in verse 28! God has given you one day in seven as a special day of rest and worship. Look up Christ's own example in Luke 4:16, and then notice God's command in Hebrews 10:25. Make sure you join a good church, and spend God's day in God's way!

'Remember the Sabbath day by keeping it holy' (Exodus 20:8).

For or against?

In this passage, two groups of people stand out because of their attitude to Christ, an issue on which there can be no sitting on the fence.

Firstly, there were those who were **against him.** In verse 2 we see that there were people who went into the synagogue not to worship but because they were 'looking for a reason to accuse Jesus'. They were so bitter that when Jesus utterly defeated them (v. 4) they began to lay plans to kill him (v. 6). In face of all the evidence that he was indeed the Son of God (vv. 7-11) they still held out against him. Today some people criticize Christ and his teaching without even putting him to the test. If only they would take the advice of Psalm 34:8, they would discover, as I am sure you are doing, that 'the Lord is good'!

The second group (about whom we read in vv. 13-19) was composed of the twelve disciples, who were **for him.** Jesus chose this small group of very ordinary men and gave them authority to preach (v. 14), and special powers to carry out the ministry committed to them (v. 15). But first of all they were chosen 'that they might be with him' (v. 14). They would never have been able to live and work as they did without first being 'with him'. As a Christian, you can rejoice that the Lord has chosen you to be his disciple (see John 15:16), but you will need to remember that this places a great responsibility upon you in your daily life. Let each day begin and end 'with him', and then seek to live in such a way that people at home, at school or at work will react as others did in Acts 4:13! None of your gifts and abilities will have as great an impact on the lives of other people as the clear evidence that you are in vital touch with the living Christ.

'No one can serve two masters . . . You cannot serve both God and Money' (Matthew 6:24).

The vital test

The first part of today's reading deals with misunderstanding, something you may have to face because you are a Christian. The second part tells of a way by which you can test the reality of your faith.

Denying God's work.   Many people misunderstood Jesus. Some of his friends said that he was mad (v. 21). Others even said that he used powers of evil to work his miracles (v. 22). Jesus' answer to this second group was simple but devastating (vv. 23-27) – how could evil powers be used to defeat themselves? He then warned them of the terrible sin of saying that a work of God was a work of the devil and of refusing to respond to the witness of the Holy Spirit concerning Jesus Christ as the Son of God (vv. 28-30). You may well find people saying that you have got 'religious mania', or that your profession of faith is a 'stunt', or in some other way not genuine. Your answer is not to hit back, but to see to it that your whole life is a constant witness to the reality of your conversion. In the words of a children's chorus, 'You can show that Christ can save, by the way that you behave'!

Doing God's will.   From a very simple incident (vv. 31-32), Jesus drew a powerful lesson, namely that we prove the reality of our relationship to him by doing God's will (v. 35). As a Christian, you are a member of God's family (see John 1:12 and Galatians 3:26). Make sure that in every part of your daily life you reveal the family likeness! Let the standard of your life be an unanswerable testimony to the work of God's grace in your heart. Look up what David said in Psalm 40:8. If you can truthfully share his testimony, you have the right foundation on which to build a solid Christian life which will stand up to sceptical criticism of any kind.

'Whoever has my commands and obeys them, he is the one who loves me'   (John 14:21).

Hearing the Word

A parable has been called 'an earthly story with a heavenly meaning'. In verses 3-9 Jesus tells one of the best-known parables in the Bible, and in verses 14-20 he explains what it means. It tells of four ways in which people hear 'the word' (v.14), that is to say, the Bible's own teaching.

The careless (vv. 4,15).   God's Word seems to make little impression on these people, and they have no sooner heard it than the devil snatches it away, and they remain unblessed. (Compare Psalm 95:7-8.)

The casual (vv. 5-6, 16-17).   These receive it 'with joy' (v. 16) but without really applying it seriously to their lives. The result is that the Word does not really take root and 'when trouble or persecution comes because of the word, they quickly fall away' (v. 17).

The carnal (vv. 7, 18-19).   These hear the Word quite clearly, but they then cram life so full of carnal, worldly things that the Word gets crowded out, with the result that it becomes 'unfruitful' (v. 19).

The careful (vv. 8, 20).   These are described as 'good soil' (v. 20), ground in which God's Word is carefully planted and tended, so that the result is a great harvest.

The lesson from all this is summed up by Jesus in verse 9, where he tells all men to pay careful attention to the Word of God. Link the 'what' of Mark 4:24 with the 'how' of Luke 8:18! If you want to be the very best for God, you will need to study the Bible regularly, earnestly and prayerfully. Determine now that you will always seek to be a careful reader of God's Word, and ask him each day to make it bear much fruit in your daily life.

'I have hidden your word in my heart that I might not sin against you' (Psalm 119:11).

Others!

As a Christian, you should be finding that you have a real concern to share the gospel with others. Today's reading tells of two ways in which you can do this.

Let it show! In verse 21 we are told that secret discipleship is not really possible. Nobody lights a candle and then puts it under a bowl or a bed! In the same way you should never be ashamed to speak up for Christ and in that way to witness for him. Notice also verse 25 – not to use a gift is to lose it! Read carefully what Jesus said about this kind of thing in Matthew 5:14-16 – and notice especially the end of verse 16. A candle does not shine to draw attention to itself but to something else. Your life should shine in such a way that people will want to know God for themselves.

Let it grow! In verses 26-29 and 30-34, Jesus tells two parables to illustrate the growth of the kingdom of God. The first shows that the growth is unseen, secret. The second shows the mighty result of this gradual growth – a tiny seed eventually becomes a massive tree. In the same way, if you nourish your faith by daily prayer and Bible study, and by regular worship, fellowship and service, you will be amazed at the number of people who have been influenced and blessed through your life and as the result of your faithful witness for Christ. What an encouragement that will be to you! But remember that first things come first, and before there is ever visible fruit there must first be the invisible root, sinking deeply down into the means which God has provided for your spiritual health and strength. To neglect them is not only to weaken your own life, but to leave many other people unblessed. Take a few moments to read the whole of Psalm 1 – and notice the clear link between verse 3 and verse 4.

'Live as children of light' (Ephesians 5:8).

Christ's authority (1)

This is a very short passage, but it tells a vivid story that can teach us many things. It can be summed up very simply in three words.

Chaos (v.37).   The disciples knew the Sea of Galilee well, but it was while crossing its familiar waters that trouble came, in the form of a squall which threatened to sink the boat. If you look up John 16:33 you will see how carefully Jesus warned his disciples that they would run into all kinds of storms as they went through life. In John 15:19 he explained why this will always happen to Christians!

Christ (v. 38).   The disciples knew exactly where to turn for help in their sudden crisis and, as always, Jesus proved himself to be the Master of the situation. Even in those circumstances, he was in complete control, as he showed by demonstrating his power over nature. Colossians 1:16 will tell you why he had this power.

Calm (v.39).   Notice the contrast between the 'furious squall' of verse 37 and the 'calm' of verse 39. This was because Jesus stepped in to deal with the situation. In their own strength the disciples were helpless; they thought they were bound to 'drown' (v. 38). When Jesus took over, the danger was past, and they must have been ashamed at what he told them in verse 40! You are bound to run into doubts and difficulties in the Christian life, and sometimes they will seem as dark and dangerous as a howling gale at sea. When you do, remember that because you are a Christian Jesus is 'in the boat' (v. 36) and that you can always call upon him for wisdom, guidance, courage and power. God has not promised that Christians will go through life without difficulties; but he *has* promised to bring them deliverance.

'All authority in heaven and on earth has been given to me' (Matthew 28:18)

Christ's authority (2)

You may find some of today's reading difficult to understand at first, but it will be a help to focus on three things said about a man who called himself 'Legion' (v. 9).

Firstly, we see him **demented.** Verses 2-5 paint a frightening picture of a demented man living in the rocky caves near the Sea of Galilee. We do not know exactly what his illness was, but we are told that he was violent, uncontrollable and self-destructive (vv. 3-5). Never under-estimate the power of Satan's forces; the Christian has to face tremendous spiritual opposition in this world. Look at what the apostle Paul has to say in Ephesians 6:12.

Secondly, we see the man **delivered.** What a contrast in the man when we come to verse 15! Once again a situation which men had given up as hopeless (see the end of v. 4) was transformed by the power of the Lord Jesus Christ. Notice that the evil spirits recognized Christ's authority over them (vv. 7,12). When the evil spirits had been cast out, 'Legion' was no longer a restless, raving madman; instead he was, as we would say today, 'cool, calm and collected'!

Lastly, we see him as a **disciple.** The man, now healed, wanted to go with Jesus (v. 18), but Jesus commanded him to go back home to his family and tell them what he had done for him (v. 19). Notice that he obeyed straight away and that the gospel spread to ten nearby cities (the meaning of 'Decapolis' in v. 20) as a result! A changed life is the best evidence of a person's conversion and the best place to show it is amongst one's closest daily contacts. Have you begun to see changes in your own life, and have people begun to notice those changes at home, at school or at work?

'Therefore, if anyone is in Christ, he is a new creation; the old has gone, the new has come!' (2 Corinthians 5:17.)

Christ's authority (3)

In this passage, we see yet again the power and authority of the Lord Jesus Christ at work.

In the first place we see that he has **authority over disease** (vv.25-34). The woman concerned had been suffering for twelve years from a haemorrhage which no doctor had been able to cure (v. 25). In her desperate condition she turned to Christ. Such was her faith that she could say, 'If I just touch his clothes I will be healed' (v. 28) and Jesus rewarded her faith with his word of authority over disease: 'Be freed from your suffering' (v. 34). Jesus is able to deal with problems that have troubled and defeated you for years, if you will only take them to him in faith.

Secondly, we see that Jesus has **authority over death** (vv. 35-43). Jesus had been on his way to the home of a religious leader called Jairus, whose twelve-year-old daughter had been seriously ill (vv. 22-24). Now, servants came to say that there was no need to trouble Jesus any further as the girl was dead (v. 35). Jesus replied, 'Don't be afraid; just believe' (v. 36) and when he got to the house he wonderfully demonstrated his authority even over death (vv. 41-42). He asked the girl to do the impossible, and with the command came the power! Whatever Jesus commands you to do, you may be sure of his power to enable you to do it. By the way, notice how Jesus is concerned about the everyday details of a person's life! (v. 43.) It is a great encouragement to know that as Christians we do not go through life alone, but that in the Lord Jesus Christ we have a living Saviour who is concerned about every detail of our lives, and able in all things to meet us at the point of our personal need. What is more, the Bible teaches that for Christians death is a 'sleep' from which God will one day awaken them and bring them into all the fulness of eternal life with him (link v. 39 with 1 Thessalonians 4:14).

'With God all things are possible' (Matthew 19:26).

The cost of refusing

Today's reading divides into two clear parts.

In the first, which takes in verses 1-6, we see **power refused.** Look at the amazing words at the beginning of verse 5! Why was it that Jesus, whose authority we have been studying for three days, 'could not do any miracles there'? The answer lies in verse 6: 'their lack of faith'. This is the terrible result of refusing to have faith in God. Christ had power to save from sickness, sorrow and sin, but the people of 'his home town' (v. 1) refused to have anything to do with him. (See John 1:11, which shows that most of the Jews rejected him.) The people of Nazareth knew him as a neighbour – were they jealous of his purity and power? They had to admit he did remarkable things (v. 2). Never set any limits on God's power in other people's lives, and never refuse him admission into any part of your own life!

In the second part of our reading we see **power received.** In verse 7 we read that when Jesus had called his disciples together he 'gave them authority over evil spirits'. The disciples were not to go around apologizing for God's message but declaring it with dignity, authority and certainty. Jesus knew that to some people the message would be offensive (v. 11), just as it had been when he had spoken it (compare v. 3). Nevertheless, the message of verse 12 had to be preached, whatever the cost. Matthew 24:14 tells us that the same responsibility is ours today. Notice, too, how completely the disciples were to rely upon God for their daily needs (vv. 8-9). Never be afraid to get involved in Christian work, and always be prepared to do *everything* God asks you to do, knowing that he will supply all that you need in order to obey his commands.

'I am not ashamed of the gospel'   (Romans 1:16).

The cost of sinning

This terrible passage centres around Herod Antipas, a ruler of part of Galilee, and helps us to see something of the seriousness of sin. Our reading tells us three things about this evil king.

His godlessness. He broke God's law by marrying his brother's wife (v. 17) and he persistently rebelled against the warnings given by God's servant, John the Baptist (v. 18). Even though verse 20 seems to show that he had some respect for John's character, at best he only trifled with the truth. While enjoying himself at a party one day he made a careless promise (v. 23) which resulted in his agreeing to John's brutal murder.

His grief. In verse 26 we read that Herod was 'greatly distressed'. But he was too proud to do the right thing, and his pride forced him on to order the execution (v. 27). No wonder the Bible says that 'The way of the unfaithful is hard' (Proverbs 13:15). Take this as a warning that one sin often leads to another!

His guilt. All this had been some time before, but Herod's conscience was at work and when he heard of the amazing things Jesus was doing he was afraid that John had miraculously risen from the dead to plague him again (vv. 14-16). As the Bible rightly reminds us, '"There is no peace," says the Lord, "for the wicked"' (Isaiah 48:22). Within a short space of time, Herod committed an even worse crime (see Luke 23:11). His story is a terrible reminder of the cost of sinning. Even though you are a Christian you can never sin cheaply, because sin will spoil your witness and rob you of your joy, assurance and effectiveness. Even more tragically, it will disrupt your fellowship with God and cause sorrow to him. Every Christian should take serious account of the cost of sinning.

'I write this to you so that you will not sin' (1 John 2:1).

The bread of life

In this section of Mark's Gospel we see the Lord Jesus Christ concerned about every part of our being – physical, mental and spiritual – and yet again we see that he is able to meet all our needs.

Physical. Notice in verses 31-32 how Jesus recognized the importance of rest and relaxation. God made our bodies, and knows all their limitations. He does not expect you to spend all your time 'coming and going' (v. 31). But neither does he want you to be lazy – notice that the disciples were only invited to take '*some* rest' (v. 31). Getting a right balance between work and leisure is an important part of growing up as a Christian. Ask God to help you in doing this so that you avoid both extremes of overwork and indolence.

Mental. In verse 34 we read that Jesus 'began teaching them many things'. Some people think that Christianity is only for the unintelligent or unfulfilled, but in fact Jesus was the greatest teacher of all time. See what men said about him in Matthew 7:28-29 and 13:54, and see how some of the religious experts of his time reacted in Luke 2:46-47! The Bible says, 'The fear [worship] of the Lord is the beginning of wisdom' (Psalm 111:10).

Spiritual. The miracle of the feeding of the five thousand was yet another demonstration of the wonder-working power of the Lord Jesus Christ. But there is another lesson here. In John's account of the same miracle, Jesus goes on to say that he himself is 'the bread of life' (John 6:35) and that a Christian's life is drawn from him (vv. 56-57). Just as physically we cannot live without food, so spiritually we cannot live without Christ. The lesson is obvious: we must draw on our spiritual resources in Christ as continually as we take in physical nourishment.

'I no longer live, but Christ lives in me' (Galatians 2:20).

God with us

In this incident Mark tells us three things about Christ which should both challenge and encourage us.

Christ's prayer. Before Jesus went into the hills to pray, he sent away not only the crowd but also the disciples (vv. 45-46). Real prayer is seldom easy and one needs to shut out anything that would distract. To realize this will help you to choose the best time and place for your daily prayers and Bible reading. Even a tiring day and a late night could not keep Jesus from this vital appointment with his heavenly Father. The disciples, meanwhile, were being blown off course by a fierce gale which swept across the Sea of Galilee. Jesus saw them in trouble (v. 48), but to test their faith, he allowed them to toil for hours (the 'fourth watch of the night' in verse 48 would mean about 3 a.m.) and even though he walked towards them on the water he made as if to pass them by. The disciples were terrified (vv. 49-50).

Christ's presence. They 'all saw him' (v. 50), but nobody recognized him! The same kind of thing happened in John 20:19-20. God's promise is 'I will never leave you nor forsake you' (Joshua 1:5). To recognize that God is with us is to bring courage and calm even in the most difficult circumstances.

Christ's power. This passage shows the power Jesus exercised over the disciples' fear (v. 50), over the storm (v. 51) and over many kinds of disease (vv. 55-56). All this reminds us that one day all his enemies will be put 'under his feet' (1 Cor. 15:25).

As a Christian you will sometimes find that life is like struggling against a strong headwind (1 John 5:19 will tell you why!) but you can take every problem to the Lord in prayer, you can be sure of Christ's presence and you can rely on his power. The Christian's resources are sufficient to overcome all of his difficulties.

'If God is for us, who can be against us' (Romans 8:31).

Ritual v. reality

In this somewhat longer passage we see two sharp contrasts being drawn. By looking at them carefully we can learn a very important lesson.

Outward ritual. The Pharisees (strict, orthodox Jews) had a host of regulations and among them were many which laid down whether a thing was ceremonially clean or unclean. These were not part of the 'commands of God' (v. 8) but were only 'tradition' (vv. 3, 5, 9, 13) or 'rules taught by men' (v. 7). Unfortunately, the Pharisees paid more attention to these outward things than to anything else, and even went so far as to leave aside God's Word in order to do so (v. 8). Religion to them meant the careful following of hundreds of petty rules and regulations, regardless of whether a person really loved God or his fellow-men. How different to the way in which Jesus summed up God's law in Matthew 22:37-40!

Inward reality. Verses 14-23 give us a clear insight into the realities of life, and tell us where sin has its root. Sin is a heart disease, not a skin complaint! Behind every word is a thought; behind every action is an attitude. A person's conduct is decided by his character. What you *do* is decided by what you *are*! Look at the terrible catalogue of sins in verses 21-22, and notice that they include sins of thought, word and deed. All of these, Jesus says, 'come from inside' (v. 23). In other words, the way a man thinks, speaks and acts does more than make him 'unclean'; it is a clear indication of the kind of person he really is. No wonder the Bible says, 'Above all else, guard your heart, for it is the wellspring of life' (Proverbs 4:23). Never judge the quality of your Christian life by outward religious activities; instead examine your heart and ensure that you are seeking to live to the glory of God.

'Man looks at the outward appearance, but the Lord looks at the heart' (1 Samuel 16:7).

Good news for all!

From these very interesting verses we can learn something about two subjects which in the goodness of God are brought together in the New Testament.

The Gentiles.   Jesus was now in Gentile (or to the Jews, pagan) country, having, it seems, gone there for a rest (v. 24). The ordinary Jew would have nothing to do with a Gentile (compare John 4:9) as he did not believe that a Gentile could ever be a member of God's kingdom. That is why, when the Greek woman – a Gentile – asked Jesus to heal her daughter, Jesus made the unusual reply in verse 27. The 'children' were the Jews; the 'dogs' were the Gentiles, and Jesus was obviously using these everyday descriptions to test the reality of the woman's faith. She replied by reminding Jesus that even the dogs had something to eat (v. 28), and he immediately honoured her faith by healing her daughter (v. 29).

The gospel.   The great lesson from this passage (which includes the healing of the deaf man who also had difficulty in speaking, vv. 32-35) is that just as Jesus wiped out the difference between clean and unclean foods (see yesterday's reading), so he wiped out the difference between Jew and Gentile. See how the apostle Paul put it in Galatians 3:26-28. The Jews were certainly God's chosen people, but they were chosen to bring the gospel of the Lord Jesus Christ to the whole world and not to keep it exclusively to themselves. No race, colour or backgound need prevent any person coming to Christ. As a Christian – part of 'the Israel of God' (Galatians 6:16) – you have been chosen to share in the great work of spreading this wonderful news throughout the whole world. Like the apostle Paul, you have been 'entrusted with the gospel' (1 Thessalonians 2:4). Be sure to take this responsibility seriously as part of God's revealed will (Mark 16:15).

'Whoever wishes, let him take the free gift of the water of life' (Revelation 22:17).

Concerned?

A few days ago we read about the miraculous feeding of five thousand people. Now Mark tells us about a similar occasion. In this incident we see several people who are concerned, though in very different ways!

The Lord's concern. Verses 1-3 again show the intense 'compassion' (v. 2) of Jesus, his deep concern for the needs of others. Matthew 9:36 is one of many other places where we see this. The disciples only had seven loaves and a few small fish (vv. 6-7), but when they were given to Jesus he was miraculously able to multiply them to supply a crowd of 4,000. However small they may seem to you, God can do great things with your gifts if you offer them to him!

The Pharisees' concern. We read about this in verses 11-13. They wanted 'a sign from heaven' to convince them that Jesus was sent from God. In spite of all his healing, teaching and preaching, they still would not believe on him. What terrible hardness of heart! Notice the tragic words 'he left them' in verse 13, and compare John 8:24.

The disciples' concern. After crossing the Sea of Galilee, the disciples found they had forgotten to take any bread (v. 14). When Jesus began to speak about 'the yeast of the Pharisees and that of Herod' (v. 15) they were even more concerned, and had a guilty conscience about their carelessness (v. 16). But Jesus showed them that they had no need to worry about bread (vv. 20,21). What he was trying to teach them was to beware of the dangers of hypocrisy ('the yeast of the Pharisees') and of worldliness ('the yeast of Herod'). Are you concerned? You ought to be – not about 'signs', nor about grasping for earthly things, but about avoiding insincerity and hypocrisy in every area of your life and about ensuring that your actions are not motivated by worldliness and self-interest.

'Seek first his kingdom and his righteousness, and all these things will be given to you as well' (Matthew 6:33).

'The Christ' (1)

In today's reading Mark gives us a three-dimensional picture of Jesus.

The Restorer of sight. What a beautiful story we have in verses 22-26! Notice once more the compassion of Jesus, and how much time he was prepared to spend with one man. The Bible teaches that he is the restorer of spiritual sight, too – see what he said in John 11:40.

The Revealer of salvation. When Jesus asked the vital question of verse 27, the disciples reported a whole variety of answers. It was Peter who openly confessed that he believed Jesus to be 'the Christ' (v. 29). The word means 'Anointed' and is the same as the word 'Messiah', the one for whom the Jews had been longing for centuries, and who would save them from their enemies and restore their nation's power. Jesus now reveals that he is this Messiah, anointed by God to be the Saviour of men. Peter could not understand why Jesus had to die in order to bring salvation, but when his ignorance led him to criticize what Jesus was doing (v. 32) it earned him a terrible rebuke (v. 33). Jesus' words mean that Peter was speaking as Satan would have done.

The Redeemer of souls. How important is a person's soul? Jesus said it was more important than the whole world! (v. 36.) In order to save it, a person must 'lose it' by yielding it completely to Christ (v. 35). Those not prepared to pay this price are given a clear warning (v. 38). Today, you are living in an 'adulterous and sinful generation'; never be ashamed to live whole-heartedly for the one who restored your spiritual sight, revealed himself as your Saviour, and redeemed your soul. 1 Peter 2:9 will help to point you in the right direction.

'A Saviour . . . Christ the Lord' (Luke 2:11).

'The Christ' (2)

Yesterday we read how Jesus revealed himself as 'the Christ'. Today, let us listen to three voices confirming that claim.

The voice of prophecy.   After he had taken Peter, James and John up on a high mountain, Jesus had become amazingly transfigured (vv. 2-3) and Moses and Elijah were seen talking to him (v. 4). Moses was the Jews' great lawgiver and Elijah was their mighty prophet. To the watching disciples, this would have been impressive proof that Jesus really did fulfil the Old Testament prophecies about God's Messiah. See what Jesus said about the Old Testament in John 5:39.

The voice of divinity.   After this, the mountain-top was covered in cloud (v. 7). In Old Testament days, the Jews often connected this with God's presence (see Exodus 16:10, for instance). From the cloud there now came God's voice, confirming that the disciples should listen to Jesus and obey him (v. 7). Later, Peter confirmed what a tremendous impact this had on them (see 2 Peter 1:16-18).

The voice of history.   On the way down the mountain-side, Jesus told the disciples to tell nobody what they had seen until 'the Son of Man had risen from the dead' (v. 9). The disciples, who thought that this would mean the end of the world, reminded Jesus of a prophecy in Malachi 4:5-6 which said that Elijah must first come. Jesus replied by saying that Elijah (John the Baptist) has *already* come to prepare the way for him and had been rejected by men and that he (Jesus) would also 'suffer much and be rejected' (v. 12). Look up Luke 23:11 and see how exactly the voice of history confirmed this. By his life, in his death, and in his resurrection, Jesus proved himself to be 'the Christ' (see Romans 1:3-4).

'My Lord and my God'   (John 20:28).

Down to earth!

These verses are in stark contrast with yesterday's reading. The story moves from the mountain to the valley, from triumph to tragedy, from delight to despair. Let us look together at three reasons why the disciples failed, and let us check our own lives at the same time.

Prayer ignored. When the disciples asked Jesus why they had failed to heal the boy (v. 28) Jesus put his finger right on the spot by saying it was because they had failed to pray. The apostle James says the same thing: 'You do not have, because you do not ask God' (James 4:2). Is this true of you in any way? One thing is certain – you cannot have victory in public unless you are vigilant in private!

Power impeded. Right back in Mark 3:14-15 Jesus had given the disciples power to 'drive out demons', but because they were disobedient over prayer the flow of power into their lives was blocked. Sin always does that, spoiling our witness (v. 14) and ruining our usefulness (v. 18). Notice, by the way, that this was a sin of omission, and look up James 4:17. Is there any unconfessed and unforsaken sin that is spoiling your life? If so, ask God to deal with it immediately.

Priorities inverted. In verse 29, some manuscripts add the words 'and fasting' after the word 'prayer' and it may be helpful to make a note of this. Fasting need not necessarily refer only to going without food, but in its wider interpretation can mean going without other things which are not wrong in themselves, but which take up time or money which would be better spent in other ways. The lesson is that a Christian should put first things first – he must get his priorities right. Check through these causes of failure very carefully, and determine that with God's help they will not be true in your life. Paul has some important words on this in Romans 12:1-2.

'Look to the Lord and his strength; seek his face always' (1 Chronicles 16:11).

Two secrets

At first glance, this passage may seem to be a strange mixture of sayings, but if you look more closely you will find that it contains at least two important truths about the Christian life.

The first is what we could call **the secret of defeat.** When they reached Capernaum, Jesus asked his disciples what they had been arguing about on the journey (v. 33). They were ashamed to tell him, because they had been arguing about which of them should be the greatest in God's kingdom (v. 34). This lies behind the three reasons for failure we noticed yesterday. The disciples were still self-centred in their ambitions and attitudes; notice how quickly they criticized the man who did not belong to their own particular circle (v. 38). In reply, Jesus took a little child in his arms as a kind of visual aid and told them that humility (v. 35), childlike trust (v. 37) and kindness (v. 41) were the marks of a true Christian. Matthew 23:12 underlines the lesson! To be self-centred always means defeat.

Next notice **the secret of victory.**   A Christian is never free from temptation; but temptation is not sin, for even Jesus was tempted (Hebrews 4:15). Many temptations, however, need not be faced if the Christian obeys the secret of victory which Jesus gives in verses 43-47. If anything you *do* ('your hand') or anywhere you *go* ('your foot') or anything you *see* ('your eye') puts temptation in your way, then cut it out! Rearrange your life so that the obvious possibility of sin is reduced to the minimum. The best time to kill a cobra is while it is still an egg! The best way to deal with sin is to cut out the things that give temptation its biggest openings. Keep a disciplined mind on what you read and watch, on where you go and on what you do. This will help you to avoid many of the heartaches of unnecessary defeat. At the same time, keep asking God to keep you from every place of danger.

'And lead us not into temptation, but deliver us from the evil one' (Matthew 6:13).

Two unchanging facts

Yesterday we learnt two important secrets of Christian living. Today's reading tells of two things which never change.

God's law.　Yet again the Pharisees were asking Jesus carefully worked out questions, aiming to trap him into making a false statement. In this case, they asked whether it was right for a man to divorce his wife (v. 2), and when Jesus asked them what Moses taught, they said that he did sometimes allow divorce. They were quite right (see Deuteronomy 24:1-4) but this was only under one condition (immorality before marriage) and, as Jesus said, it was only permitted because of the hardness of the Israelites' hearts (v. 5). It was not God's *best* for his people, and in any case did nothing to change God's first principle, laid down in Genesis 2:24 and now confirmed by Jesus (vv. 6-9). God's laws never change (see Matthew 5:17-18) and one of the things which he demands from his people is that they should honour their vows.

God's love.　The delightful incident in verses 13-16 shows perhaps more than any other the great tenderness of Jesus. It also shows that nobody is too unimportant for Jesus to love. These children meant nothing to most of the people there at that moment – even the disciples felt that the Lord's time was too valuable to be spent on them (v. 13) – yet Jesus was prepared to lavish his care and kindness on them one by one. What is more, he said that men must have the simple faith of little children if they are to enter the kingdom of God (vv. 14-15). The picture of the eternal Son of God taking children in his arms is very beautiful, but is also very powerful, reminding us of God's promise that all of his children are held in his protecting care (see Deuteronomy 33:27).

'*I the Lord do not change*'　(Malachi 3:6).

The danger of 'things'

We read today the vivid story of a very important young man (see Luke 18:18) and the great truth which Jesus taught from it.

Look closely at what Jesus said, and see first **the limit he touched.** The young man who came to him was earnest and respectful – he ran to Jesus and fell on his knees before him (v. 17). What is more, he was clearly leading a very good life, for when Jesus listed six of what we call the Ten Commandments, he was able to make the startling reply of verse 20! But then Jesus touched the limit of his goodness, for when he challenged him to give up all his wealth the young man turned away 'sad' (v. 22). He wanted to be a Christian (look at his question in v. 17) but not if it meant giving up all the things which his wealth had bought for him. But this meant that he was breaking the very first of the commandments (look it up in Exodus 20:3).

Now turn back to Jesus and notice **the lesson he taught.** In verses 23-25 Jesus said that it was very hard for a rich man to enter the kingdom of God. The disciples were 'amazed' (vv. 24,26), for many Jews believed that if a man was rich it meant that he had found favour with God. What Jesus taught was that it was dangerously easy for a man to be so interested in 'things' that he forgot all about God! When Peter reminded him that the disciples had given up a great deal in order to follow him, Jesus made the promise of verses 29-30, and added that on the Day of Judgement many people who thought they were 'first' would be 'last' – and vice versa! (v. 31.) The lesson for you? Beware of getting too involved with 'things'; remember that spiritual values are of first importance; put Christ first in every part of your life. No amount of possessions can take the place of a vital and deepening relationship with God. See what God says in Proverbs 11:28.

'Though your riches increase, do not set your heart on them' (Psalm 62:10).

Towards Jerusalem

Jesus had now set his face firmly towards Jerusalem (v. 32), although he knew that it would mean his death.

On the way, he began to tell the disciples about **the vision of suffering.** Twice before in Mark's Gospel Jesus had forecast his death (look up 8:31 and 9:31). Now he gave some of the terrible details, all of which came true. Jesus wanted to make it quite clear that only by dying could he become the Saviour of the world. Notice the clear statement in verse 45. A 'ransom' is a price paid to deliver a person from slavery or captivity.

Yet even after hearing Jesus forecast the appalling suffering he was to undergo, at least two of the disciples were still **the victims of self.** While Jesus was concerned with dying for others, James and John were only concerned about their own positions (v. 37). The question in verse 38 simply means: 'Can you go through what I am going to suffer?' and their brash answer was 'We can'! (v. 39.) Jesus then told them that they *would* in fact suffer for their faith (Acts 12:2 and Revelation 1:9 tell us how right he was) but that heaven's rewards were in God the Father's hands.

When the other disciples rebuked James and John, Jesus took the opportunity of teaching all of them **the value of serving.** In ordinary life, Jesus said, men liked to lord it over each other (v. 42), but Christians should show humility and a willingness to serve (vv. 43-44). Jesus then gave himself as the great example, and in the wonderful words of verse 45 he summed up his whole mission on earth, which was not to *get* but to *give* – eventually to give his life as a ransom for sinful men. Think little of yourself, think much of others and remember that a Christian should be one who is willing to serve his fellow men. Paul puts your responsibility very clearly in Galatians 6:10.

'Serve one another in love' (Galatians 5:13).

Jesus makes whole

The astonishing miracle described in today's reading began with a man called Bartimaeus sitting by the roadside. Three things about him hold the story together.

His pathetic condition. Two tragic words in verse 46 tell us this – he was 'blind' and 'begging'. This is a vivid picture of people who are not Christians, though many do not realize their condition – see how the apostle Paul puts it in 2 Corinthians 4:4. To be without Christ is to be helpless and hopeless. As Christians, we must always be concerned for those who are in this pathetic condition as the result of their sinful nature and behaviour.

His persistent cry. Bartimaeus heard that Jesus was passing by and he began to cry out for help (v. 47). When people tried to stop him, he shouted even louder (v. 48). He was determined that nothing would stop him making his need known to Jesus – not even his cloak (v. 50)! The Bible teaches us that we should not just pray but *keep on praying*. Jesus told a parable about this at the beginning of Luke 18. See, too, what Paul says in 1 Thessalonians 5:17.

His perfect cure. Bartimaeus knew exactly what his need was (v. 51), and because of his great faith, Jesus met it completely, and we read that 'he received his sight' (v. 52). The result was that he no longer sat beside the highway begging; instead, he 'followed Jesus along the road' (v. 52). There is a lesson here. As you come to Jesus in prayer, and find your needs met by him, never be content to go on living as you did before. Step out with the Master into the fulness of life which he has planned and prepared for you. You can see what kind of life this is meant to be if you look up John 10:10. The Christian life is meant to be one of fulness and progress.

'Grow in the grace and knowledge of our Lord and Saviour Jesus Christ' (2 Peter 3:18).

When Jesus comes

Today we read the story of Jesus entering Jerusalem, but for the sake of tidiness we shall not study verses 12-14 until tomorrow. Once again, Jesus is the centre of our attention.

His royal acclaim. Jesus deliberately chose to ride into Jerusalem on a donkey. This was to show the people quite clearly that he was their Messiah; they would remember what God had said through his prophet in Zechariah 9:9. Look it up, and notice how accurate the Bible is! As soon as they knew what Jesus meant, they went wild with excitement, and gave him what we might call 'the red carpet treatment'! (vv. 7-8.) 'He who comes' (v. 9) is another expression the Jews used for 'Messiah', and the word 'Hosanna' (vv. 9-10) meant 'Save now!' In their wild enthusiasm, the people believed that Jesus was about to overthrow the Roman authorities, take control of the city by force and set up an earthly kingdom.

His righteous anger. As soon as Jesus reached the city he went to the temple and looked carefully around (v. 11). The following day he went back there and immediately began to take drastic action! (v. 15.) People were using the temple as a market-place (v. 15); others were just using it as a short-cut from one part of the city to another (v. 16); money-changers were swindling the pilgrims (v. 17). Jesus swept all of these out of the temple, reminding them that God intended it to be a holy place, a place set aside for worship and prayer. Check verse 17 with Jeremiah 7:11. It is right to welcome Jesus as King, for so he is, but always remember that as King he has the right to reign, and this may sometimes mean changing things that have gone on for years. Let Jesus have complete control of your life and be prepared to have things disturbed! Think through the implications of Isaiah 55:8,9.

'Jesus Christ is Lord' (Philippians 2:11).

Anything missing?

If we link verses 12-14 with today's short reading, we can trace three things that are missing, or absent.

We begin with missing **fruit.** Notice how Mark describes the fig tree. He says it had 'nothing but leaves' (v. 13) although it should also have had an early crop of fruit. This was a vivid picture of the Jewish nation at the time, because although it had a great deal of outward religion it was not producing spiritual fruit. Jesus always said that the reality of man's religion could be judged by whether or not there was spiritual fruit (see Matthew 7:20, for instance). The sentence which Jesus passed on the tree (v. 14) swiftly came to pass (v. 20) – a solemn warning about the need to be *sure* that we are right with God.

The second missing thing was **faith.** Peter was amazed that the fig tree *had* actually withered (v. 21), but Jesus replied by saying that, with the weapon of believing prayer, difficulties and problems which might seem to be as large as mountains could be removed. As God teaches you to pray, learn to *trust* him for the answers.

Yet before it can be genuine and effective the prayer of faith must be accompanied by **forgiveness.** In verses 25-26, Jesus made it clear that we shall need to forgive others if we ourselves want to be forgiven. When Jesus taught the disciples what we now call the Lord's Prayer, this was the one thing which he repeated and emphasized. You can check on this by reading Matthew 6:9-15. God is love, and we cannot have fellowship in prayer with him while we ourselves have an unforgiving spirit towards others. Bitterness in your heart can be a real hindrance to answered prayer. Ask God now to remove any such hindrance and to give you the grace to forgive anybody who has wronged you in any way. Ephesians 4:32 will give you the perfect reason for doing so.

'Forgive, and you will be forgiven' (Luke 6:37).

The Master (1)

The opposition to Jesus was gradually increasing, but he remained the complete Master of every situation.

In today's reading he begins by posing *a searching problem.* The religious rulers asked him what authority he had to cleanse the temple (v. 28). He replied that he would tell them if they would first tell him whether John the Baptist's ministry was inspired by God or men (v. 30). Now they were cornered! If they said John was a true prophet, then Jesus would ask them why they did not believe what John said about him (in John 1:29, for instance). If they said John was a false prophet, they knew the crowd would attack them, for John was held in high esteem (v. 32). Verse 33 neatly describes their defeat!

Jesus then told them *a striking parable.* To understand the parable, we must identify the characters. The 'man' (v. 1) was God; the 'vineyard' (v. 1) was the Jewish nation; the 'farmers' (v. 1) were the rulers; the 'servants' (vv. 2,4,5) were the Old Testament prophets. Here was the story about God's goodness to their nation (look at v. 1 again) and of the way in which time and again they had rejected God's messengers. Finally, God sent his Son (v. 6), with the terrible result described in verses 7-8 – a clear prophecy of Jesus' death. But the story does not end there. Verse 9 was a forecast that Jerusalem would be destroyed (and it was, about forty years later) and verses 10-11 (check with Psalm 118:22-23) were a prophecy that Jesus would one day rise from the dead, becoming 'the capstone' (v. 10), supreme throughout all ages. The authorities knew that the parable condemned them and slunk away, ashamed and defeated (v. 12). Even when whole nations seem to reject him and overthrow his purposes, Jesus remains supreme. Read the whole of Psalm 2 for a brilliant summary of what the Bible says about this.

'He is Lord of lords and King of kings'   (Revelation 17:14).

The Master (2)

Still the questions came – and still Jesus was the Master!

The next to test him were the Pharisees and members of a political group called the Herodians (v. 13), who asked *a question about everyday loyalty.* The question was simple enough: was it right for the Jews to pay taxes to the Romans, who were occupying their country at that time? But again there was a catch in it. If Jesus said 'Yes', the people would say he was disloyal to the Jews; if he said 'No', they would report him to the Romans. Jesus gave a simple but shattering answer (vv. 16-17). The lesson for us is this: as Christians we should be good citizens, willing to abide by the laws which are made for our benefit and protection, and willing to pay taxes which are lawfully due and which go towards providing many benefits for ourselves and others (read Romans 13:1-7). But notice that Jesus also pointed out that men have a greater loyalty – to God. We are made 'in his own *image*' (Genesis 1:27) and rightly belong to him.

The next to challenge Jesus were the Sadducees (v. 18), who did not believe in the resurrection. They asked *a question about eternal life.* They invented a fantastic story about a woman who married each of seven brothers in turn and became a widow seven times over (vv. 20-22), and asked Jesus whose wife she would be after the resurrection (v. 23). In reply, Jesus first of all told them that after this life there is no such thing as marriage, as it is a different kind of life altogether (v. 25). He then took the opportunity to prove to them from the writings of Moses (which they believed to be true) that the resurrection was a *fact* (read vv. 26-27, and check this with Exodus 3:6). One last point: notice *why* Jesus said they made such a bad mistake: 'because you do not know the Scriptures' (v. 24). Study God's Word if you want to know God's way!

'The statutes of the Lord are trustworthy, making wise the simple' (Psalm 19:7).

The Master (3)

In four quick sketches, Mark continues to show us the Master at work during that remarkable day at Jerusalem.

The scribe he convinced.   Jesus answered the scribe's sincere question (v. 28) by linking together two Old Testament phrases (check vv. 29-31 with Deuteronomy 6:4-5 and Leviticus 19:18). The scribe was completely convinced that Jesus had spoken the truth and went on to agree that to love God with one's whole being was the most important thing in life (vv. 32-33). No wonder Jesus said that he was 'not far from the kingdom of God'! (v. 34.) The scribe was convinced; I wonder if he was ever converted.

The scripture he considered.   The scribes and others (see Matthew 9:27, for instance) called the Messiah 'the son of David' (v. 35) because they believed he would be born into King David's family. Jesus now asks them to consider the first verse of Psalm 110 (written by David), in which David refers to the coming Messiah as 'my Lord' (v. 36). Yet again, Jesus was trying to show the people, from their beloved Old Testament, that he was in fact the Son of God, the expected Messiah.

The sham he condemned.   This was carried on by some of the scribes, who offered 'lengthy prayers' (v. 40), but who beneath all the outward show of religion were inwardly proud (vv. 38-39) and greedy (v. 40).

The sacrifice he commended.   Finally, Jesus watched the temple visitors placing gifts into the collecting boxes (v. 41). Some rich people put in 'large amounts', but although the widow only put in two coins – worth only a fraction of a penny – it was in fact 'all she had to live on' (v. 44) and she earned the Lord's commendation (v. 43). Nothing you are, or have, is hidden from God. Do you honour him in your living, and in your giving?

'Lord, you know all things'   (John 21:17).

Christ's second coming (1)

One of the most wonderful promises Jesus made is found in John 14:3, where he said, 'I will come back.' This tremendous statement is part of the Bible's clear teaching that Jesus will one day return to earth, and although a good deal of the teaching on the subject is difficult to understand fully, we do know that it all leads up to God's final triumph over evil (read 1 Corinthians 15:20-28). In this chapter Jesus tells us certain things about the period leading up to his return to the earth, and for the next three days we will look at some of them. In today's reading, for instance, we can notice three things of which Jesus prophesied.

First he warned of **destruction.** When a disciple drew his attention to the magnificent temple (v. 1) Jesus made a terrible forecast (v. 2). (This actually happened in A.D. 70, when the Romans destroyed it.)

When four disciples asked Jesus when these things would happen (v. 4), Jesus went further, and prophesied even greater **disasters.** The world (v. 7), the nations (v. 8) and individual Christians (v. 9) would all be involved in these. Even within families there would be strife (v. 12). All these things are happening in the world today, and many people believe that these are signs that 'the Lord's coming is near' (James 5:8).

But notice that Jesus also promised **deliverance.** Whatever persecution the Christian might have to face, he could rely on the Holy Spirit to guide and inspire him (v. 11) and eventually the gospel would be preached throughout the world (v. 10). Finally, there is God's promise of complete deliverance to the person who by the grace of God 'stands firm to the end' (v. 13). The Lord's return draws nearer every day. Be resolute – and ready!

'This same Jesus . . . will come back' (Acts 1:11).

Christ's second coming (2)

Jesus continued to link the prophecies about the destruction of Jerusalem with the things that would happen before he came to earth again.

Notice firstly **the picture of horror.** The 'abomination that causes desolation' (check v. 14 with Daniel 9:27) would sound terrible to the Jews, for it spoke of the time when the Romans would destroy the holy city of Jerusalem and desecrate the temple. Jesus told them how to escape this terrible event (vv. 14-18) and what would happen to those who did not (v. 19). This is exactly what took place just over thirty years later. Over a million people died, and only those who fled to the mountains escaped the horror of the besieged city.

Jesus then went on to warn the disciples (and us) about **the peril of heresy.** Heresy means false teaching and in verses 21-23 Jesus repeated the warning of verse 6 and said that before he returned to the earth there would be many who would make false claims, so that people would say, 'Here is the Christ' (compare v. 21 with v. 6). We can see this happening today, with false sects springing up and deceiving people with their wrong teaching and false claims. Beware of heresy! Remember that Jesus himself is 'the way and the truth and the life' (John 14:6).

Finally today, we can take courage from **the promise of hope.** We may not be able to understand the terrible words of verses 24-25, but we do know that Jesus himself *will* return, and that it will be 'with great power and glory' (v. 26). From every part of the world he will gather 'his elect' (v. 27). This is one of the great Bible words used to describe Christians; look it up in 1 Peter 1:1-2 for instance. We may not know what the future holds, but we do know who holds the future and we can rejoice in the certainty of God's promise in 1 Thessalonians 4:15-18!

'We eagerly await . . . the Lord Jesus Christ'   (Philippians 3:20).

Christ's second coming (3)

With today's reading we complete our three days' study of this great chapter on the second coming of Christ.

The truth.　The fact that Jesus *will* come again is one of the most certain things that Scripture tells us. It is mentioned about 300 times in the New Testament alone! Jesus made it quite plain in verse 31 that every word he spoke on the subject would come to pass. Notice, too, what the disciples were later told in Acts 1:11. The Bible leaves us in no doubt that the return of Jesus Christ to this earth is a historical certainty.

The time.　Many people have tried to forecast the actual date on which Jesus will return, but all of them have been proved wrong. Jesus did say that there would be signs that his coming was near (vv. 28-29), but he also made it very clear that only God the Father knows exactly when that great day will be (v. 32).

The task.　We know that Jesus *is* coming; we do not know *when* he is coming. What should we do? The answer is clearly given in the urgent commands Jesus gives in this passage: 'Be on guard!' (v. 33); 'Be alert!' (v. 33); 'Keep watch' (v. 35); 'Watch!' (v. 37). If a famous person promised to visit your house soon, but did not give a definite date, you would make sure that you were *always* ready. As a Christian, you should be living for Jesus day by day, serving him in every way you can, looking for that wonderful day when he will take you to be with him for ever. Every part of your life should be geared to the fact that it might suddenly be interrupted by the Lord's return. See how the apostle John puts it in 1 John 2:28. Make sure that you are ready to welcome the King if he should return during your lifetime!

'It will be good for those servants whose master finds them watching when he comes' (Luke 12:37).

The clouds gather

In this chapter we shall read together some of the events leading up to Christ's crucifixion. In today's reading, three words sum up the attitudes of three people and lead us to ask three important questions.

Grace. In Palestine, it was the custom to sprinkle a few drops of perfume on an honoured guest, but when Jesus went to Simon's house for a meal, a woman there broke open a whole jar of pure nard, a very expensive perfume (v. 3). When some of the guests said this was a waste of money – notice that it was worth more than a year's wages! – Jesus commended the woman (v. 6) and said that wherever the gospel was preached her story would be told (v. 9). Are you willing to serve Jesus faithfully whatever the cost?

Greed. But this lovely story is surrounded by the gathering clouds of danger (vv. 1-2, 10-11). The chief priests and scribes were determined to trap Jesus and kill him (v. 1) and Judas Iscariot had turned into a traitor (v. 10). At one time, he must have seemed to be a true disciple, but greed had turned his heart away (compare v. 11 with John 12:6). Are you holding back from Jesus anything that rightly belongs to him?

Gratitude. Meanwhile, preparations were going on for the great Jewish festival known as the Passover (vv. 12-16). Up to three million people came to Jerusalem each year for this great event, held to celebrate the way in which God had delivered the Jewish nation from captivity in Egypt hundreds of years before. (You can read the story in Exodus 12, and especially vv. 13-14.) In the midst of danger and darkness, Jesus had time to lead his disciples in an act of gratitude. Are you continually grateful to God for all his goodness to you? Colossians 1:12-14 underlines the point.

'Give thanks in all circumstances' (1 Thessalonians 5:18).

The Lord's Supper

This passage tells us how Jesus instituted the service we call the Lord's Supper or the Holy Communion. There are three highlights here.

A cross.   It was now Thursday evening, and Jesus knew that in just a few hours he would be arrested and killed, having first been betrayed by one of those sitting at table with him (vv. 18-20). Later on (v. 27) when he said that *all* the disciples would forsake him, Peter boasted that he never would (vv. 29, 31), but as we shall see later on, he too failed his Master. The Bible says that 'all have sinned' (Romans 3:23) and that when Jesus died on the cross he died 'for the sins of the whole world' (1 John 2:2).

A covenant.   As the meal went on, Jesus took the bread and said, 'This is my body' (v. 22) and then as he shared the cup of wine with the disciples he said, 'This is my blood' (v. 24). By this, he showed them that, just as he broke the bread and poured out the wine for them that night, so the following day his real body would be given and his actual blood 'poured out for many', establishing a 'covenant' or agreement (v. 24). The 'old covenant' is in Exodus 24:3-8, where you will see that it called for man's perfect obedience. As we know, man did *not* obey, so God now made a new covenant, in which Jesus came to earth, lived a perfect life, and then offered it up as a sacrifice for the sins of others so that all who trust in him are forgiven and made right with God. If you read 1 Corinthians 11:23-29 you will see that Christians are to hold the Lord's Supper in obedience to Christ's wish (vv. 24-25) and in remembrance of his life and death.

A crown.   Notice verse 28! It begins, 'But after I have risen . . .' Beyond the cross, Jesus saw a crown; and the Bible says that by faith 'We see Jesus . . . crowned with glory and honour' (Hebrews 2:9).

'Do this is remembrance of me'   (Luke 22:19).

Gethsemane

This scene in the Garden of Gethsemane is one of the most solemn in the whole Bible. We can use three words to sum up the attitudes of the people who were there.

Willingness. This is the word we can use about Jesus. Verses 33-34 show the terrible strain he felt as he approached death. His prayer in verses 35-36 does not mean that he was afraid of dying, but that he shrank from the terrible experience of bearing the burden of the world's sin upon his sinless soul. The one who knew no sin of his own was about to be made sin for us (2 Corinthians 5:21). We shall never be able to understand the love that made Jesus willing to bear sin's penalty on our behalf (look at the end of v. 36).

Weakness. When Jesus returned to the disciples, he found them asleep (v. 37). Peter had said that he was willing to die for Jesus (look back to v. 31), yet he could not even keep awake for him! How easy it is to boast! But we need to remember that 'The body is weak' (v. 38) and that it is only as we trust in the Lord moment by moment that we can have victory over the world, the flesh and the devil (1 John 5:4).

Wickedness. Even as Jesus was speaking to his disciples, Judas Iscariot came into the garden with a crowd of people, armed to the teeth (v. 43). Acting according to a pre-arranged plan (v. 44), he betrayed Jesus with a token of love (v. 45). Such is the power of Satan! Jesus was swiftly arrested (v. 46) and although Peter was prepared to put up a bit of a fight (compare v. 47 with John 18:10) all the disciples finally ran away (v. 50). Contrast verse 50 with Luke 5:11! Man's wickedness was about to do its worst. The passage has many lessons for us and one of the most important is that we should never boast in our own strength. Romans 7:18 puts things in perspective!

'Be on your guard; stand firm in the faith; be men of courage; be strong' (1 Corinthians 16:13).

On trial (1)

We now come to two of the trials which Jesus had to stand; in the first of these he was faced by the Jewish religious leaders and in the second by the Roman civil authorities. Today's reading covers the first trial.

Courage.   The people mentioned in verse 53 formed the Jewish Sanhedrin (or Council), which had power to deal with religious matters. The law required that at least two witnesses must give evidence which agreed (look up Deuteronomy 17:6), but in this case even the carefully chosen false witnesses contradicted each other! (vv. 55-59.) Finally, the high priest asked Jesus a point-blank question (v. 61). Calmly and confidently Jesus made it quite clear that he claimed to be the Son of God (v. 62). That was just what the high priest wanted, and the whole Council found Jesus guilty of blasphemy against God, which carried an automatic death sentence (v. 64). But neither that nor the savage attack which followed (v. 65) could break the courage of Jesus.

Cowardice.   Meanwhile, Peter had found his way into the courtyard (v. 54). As he sat around the open fire a servant girl recognized him (v. 67). He quickly said he did not understand what she meant and moved away (v. 68). Again he was identified as a disciple (v. 69) but once more he denied having anything to do with Jesus (v. 70). A little while later several other people recognized his Galilean accent (v. 70). Frightened that he too might be arrested, Peter told a downright lie (v. 71), and as soon as he had done so he heard a cock crow for the second time (v. 72). With bitter shame he remembered what Jesus had said (see v. 30). Jesus on trial showed amazing courage; Peter was a coward. You will find yourself 'on trial' many times as a Christian. Never be ashamed to speak up for your Saviour. Look up what Paul says in 2 Timothy 1:7-9.

'The Lord is with me; I will not be afraid'   (Psalm 118:6).

On trial (2)

In today's reading we move on to the second trial which Jesus had to face.

The charge. From the Sanhedrin, Jesus was taken to Pilate, the Roman governor (v. 1). The Jews knew that Pilate would not be interested in a religious charge (blasphemy) so they said that Jesus was accused of setting himself up as King of the Jews, something that would obviously offend the Roman authorities. When Pilate asked him if this was true, Jesus openly admitted that it was (compare v. 2 with John 18:33-37). The chief priests now invented one charge after another (v. 3), but through it all Jesus remained silent and dignified (vv. 4-5). Pilate was amazed (v. 5), especially as he knew the real reason why Jesus had been arrested (v. 10). How do you react when you are criticized or wrongly accused? It is so easy to lose your temper, or fight back, but the Christian's attitude should be the same as that of Jesus, who 'when they hurled their insults at him . . . did not retaliate' (1 Peter 2:23).

The choice. At the Passover, there was a custom which allowed one prisoner to be set free (v. 6). Pilate saw this as an ideal chance to release the innocent Jesus (v. 9). But the chief priests stirred up the crowd to ask for the release of Barabbas, who was a rebel and murderer (vv. 7, 11). When Pilate asked them what he should do with Jesus, the crowd repeatedly shouted, 'Crucify him!' (vv. 13-14). So, although he knew that Jesus was innocent, Pilate ordered him to be whipped and crucified, just 'to satisfy the crowd' (v. 15). The crowd had to choose between Jesus and Barabbas, and they chose Barabbas; Pilate had to choose between the right thing and the easy thing, and he chose the easy thing. As a Christian, you have decided to follow Jesus. Make sure that in all of life's other decisions you do the thing which will please *him*, whatever it costs *you*. You will find the perfect example in John 8:29.

'We must obey God rather than men'   (Acts 5:29).

The cross (1)

When the second trial was over, the soldiers wasted no time in preparing to carry out the sentence.

But first they subjected Jesus to **mockery.** The purple robe and the crown of thorns (v. 17), the salute (v. 18) and the false homage (v. 19) were all sheer mockery in which all the soldiers took part (v. 16).

Little did they know the great truth at which they mocked, for throughout all this shameful experience, Jesus revealed his **majesty.** Six times in this chapter Jesus is called 'King' (vv. 2, 9, 18, 26, 32) – and so he is! (See 1 Timothy 6:13-15.) That being so, what amazing restraint Jesus showed on that terrible day, when for your sake and mine he allowed himself to be mocked, scourged and spat upon!

Now the story moves swiftly outside of the city to a place called 'Golgotha' (v. 22). This was a well-known place for holding public executions. Now it was to be the scene of Christ's **murder.** The soldiers offered Jesus a pain-killer but he refused to have his senses dulled as he faced the great crisis (v. 23) and at 'the third hour' (9 o'clock in the morning) they crucified him (v. 25). Between two criminals (v. 27) the sinless Son of God hung on a rough wooden cross, held there by huge nails driven through his hands and his feet. Meanwhile, the soldiers callously gambled for his clothes, which had been stripped from him before the crucifixion (v. 24). Horrible as all these things were, John tells us that they had been prophesied in the Word of God hundreds of years before (compare v. 24 with John 19:24 and Psalm 22:18). The cross was not an afterthought on God's part; Jesus was 'the Lamb that was slain from the creation of the world' (Revelation 13:8). Notice carefully how Luke puts this vitally important truth in Acts 2:22-23.

'He was pierced for our transgressions'   (Isaiah 53:5).

The cross (2)

In today's solemn reading we shall look together at two central things about the crucifixion of the Lord Jesus.

The meaning of his desertion. Throughout the long hours on the cross, passers-by and others mocked and teased him (vv. 29-32). Then at 'the sixth hour' (12 noon) it suddenly became as dark as night (v. 33). After three hours of eerie darkness Jesus uttered the terrible cry of verse 34. What do the words mean? The Bible says that God hates sin, and cannot even look upon it (Habakkuk 1:13). But it also says that Jesus 'bore our sins in his body on the tree' (1 Peter 2:24). Paul puts it in even stronger words when he says that God 'made him who had no sin to be sin for us' (2 Corinthians 5:21). Now the result of sin is separation from God (Isaiah 59:2) so that when Jesus took our sin God the Father had to turn away from him, exposing him to his divine wrath and judgement. We can never fully understand this, but at least we can be eternally grateful that Jesus was prepared to pay in full the terrible penalty which our sin deserved.

The moment of his death. After hours of suffering, Jesus finally 'breathed his last' (v. 37). This means that of his own free will he gave up his life. The Bible says that he 'became obedient to death' (Philippians 2:8). No man ever lived as he lived, and no man ever died as he died. No wonder a Roman soldier made such an astonishing comment! (v. 39.) Back in the city, priests who were in the temple at the time were amazed to see the huge curtain which surrounded the holy of holies suddenly torn in two from top to bottom (v. 38) – a wonderful sign from God that the way into the kingdom of heaven was now open to all who would put their trust in Christ as the one all-sufficient sacrifice for their sin.

'*The Son of God, who loved me and gave himself for me*' (Galatians 2:20).

The cross (3)

The terrible story of Christ's brutal murder now comes to a close. Let us take two final looks at it.

The solemn grief. With great tenderness, Mark tells us the names of some of the mourners (vv. 40-41). Another person who was filled with grief was a man called Joseph, who came from Arimathea, and was a member of the Council (v. 43). At the risk of revealing that he, too, was a disciple, he went to Pilate and boldly asked for the body of Jesus (v. 43). Pilate sent a soldier to make absolutely sure that Jesus was in fact dead before giving the necessary permission (v. 45). Notice the courage and the kindness of Joseph – two fine examples for every Christian to follow.

The silent grave. Verse 46 describes the last sad scenes. Joseph took the body of Jesus down from the cross, wrapped it in fine linen cloth and laid it reverently in a sepulchre, which was a cave carved out of the solid rock. A huge boulder was then rolled into position across the mouth of the cave (v. 46). From time to time people have tried to argue that Jesus never actually died on the cross, but all four Gospels make it clear beyond all possible doubt that Jesus died and was buried (see Matthew 27:62-66). The Christian faith rests on solid facts, not on sentimental feelings. Two silent witnesses made a careful note of exactly where the tomb was so that they could return later to anoint the body as a last act of love and devotion (v. 47). Joseph and the others made their way from the garden where the tomb was. Darkness fell over the great city of Jerusalem. For thousands of people, all that had happened was that the career of a man called Jesus had come to an end on a wooden cross. But before long something was to happen which would show that the death of Christ stood at the very centre of history.

'Christ died for our sins according to the Scriptures' (1 Corinthians 15:3).

He is risen!

These eight verses contain the greatest news the world has ever heard – that Jesus Christ rose from the dead and is alive for evermore!

However, this first Easter Day began in a very ordinary way, with *a problem faced.* The two Marys, having rested on the Sabbath day, bought spices to anoint the body of Jesus (v. 1). As the sun rose over the nearby hills, they made their way to the tomb (v. 2). But they had a problem: who would roll away the massive stone from the mouth of the cave? (v. 3.) Imagine their surprise when they arrived there to find it already rolled away (v. 4) and their shock in seeing an angel sitting inside the cave! (v. 5.)

From the angel's lips came the stupendous news of *a prophecy fulfilled.* The angel's message was wonderfully simple – and simply wonderful! Jesus was no longer dead, but 'risen' (v. 6). Furthermore, the angel added, 'He is going ahead of you into Galilee. There you will see him, just as he told you' (v. 7). Look back to Mark 14:28 and you will see that that is exactly what Jesus had said he would do! The women were so bewildered that they turned and ran, too frightened to tell anyone what they had seen and heard (v. 8). But nothing could hold back the truth for long – Jesus had defeated the powers of sin and death; prophecy had been wonderfully fulfilled; his Word was true; Jesus was 'declared with power to be the Son of God by his resurrection from the dead' (Romans 1:4). The fact of the resurrection of Jesus is central to the whole Christian faith, for it is proof that God accepted his death as the penalty for the sins of others. It also means that for all who put their trust in him, Jesus is not merely a historical example but a living Saviour! To grasp something of what this means, look up Paul's exhilarating words in Ephesians 1:18-21.

'God raised us up with Christ' (Ephesians 2:6).

The Lord is King

These verses were almost certainly not part of Mark's original Gospel, but they are undoubtedly part of God's Word, as similar words are recorded elsewhere in the New Testament, and we can safely include them in our studies.

A trust confirmed. With his death, the disciples' faith in Jesus as the Messiah had been shattered, and they were slow to trust the first reports of his resurrection (link vv. 10-13 with Luke 24:11), but eventually Jesus put the matter beyond all doubt (v. 14). Their trust had been confirmed in the most wonderful way possible, and they must have felt ashamed at their earlier doubts.

A task committed. Take verse 15 to heart! It is a word to all Christians for all time (compare 2 Corinthians 5:18). God has committed to us the tremendous task of telling the whole world about the salvation which comes through faith in Jesus Christ (v. 16), and as we obey him so he will give evidence that he is working with us (v. 20).

A triumph completed. As we come to the end of these studies our last thoughts must be centred around Christ himself, whose work on earth was now triumphantly completed. Some days later he ascended into heaven (read Acts 1:1-11) and, as the Bible says, 'sat at the right hand of God' (v. 19). This speaks of power and authority, and reminds us once again that he is 'King of kings and Lord of lords' (Revelation 19:16). Acknowledge him as Lord of *your* life, and determine to live each day in obedience to his will. Say with the hymn-writer:

> The Lord is King! I own his power,
> His right to rule each day and hour,
> I own his claim on heart and will,
> And his demands I would fulfil!

'In all your ways acknowledge him, and he will make your paths straight' (Proverbs 3:6).

Notes

Notes

Notes

Notes

Other books by
John Blanchard
available from
Evangelical Press

LUKE COMES ALIVE !

Sixty-two guide-lines for personal Bible reading through the Gospel of Luke.

Both stimulating and challenging, this series of notes is designed to explain Luke's Gospel and to help you see its relevance to your everyday living.

Outline expositions and pithy comments make *Luke Comes Alive!* ideal for discussion groups and Bible studies as well as personal reading.

HOW TO ENJOY YOUR BIBLE

John Blanchard believes that Christians are meant to *enjoy* the Bible, and that reading the Scriptures should be an exciting adventure into God's truth and purposes for our lives.

So how can we enjoy God's Word and avoid the trap of our Bible study being a dull, boring duty? In this excellent book, the author, an internationally known preacher and evangelist, shows us how this can be achieved.

"Simple, vivid, accurate, warm, practical and searching, it is all that we have come to expect of its author."

J.I.Packer

"It is ideally written for the young convert, has much to teach the mature Christian and is suitable for Bible study groups of every kind." **Rev. Kenneth Paterson**

LEARNING AND LIVING

How does a person become a Christian, and what is involved in living the Christian life? In answering these two questions the author directs the reader to the Bible, guiding him through God's message of salvation and explaining the tough, but exhilarating challenge of living the Christian life in today's threatening world.

"John Blanchard's blend of clarity, humour and balanced insight makes for compulsive reading."

Dedication Magazine

"This is a great book. I shall have it with me continually."

Dr Eric Hutchings

WHAT IN THE WORLD IS A CHRISTIAN?

In these days of religious confusion many people are asking, "What in the world is a Christian?" Because of a lack of teaching, or a superficial approach to Scripture, or a restless chasing after mystical "experiences" they are unable to give an adequate answer to this question.

In this revised edition of his book, John Blanchard attempts to do so. The author is convinced that there is no substitute for straightforward biblical teaching in order to produce healthy, balanced and progressive Christians.

"For the person who has never discovered Christian faith, for the early disciple in doctrine, for the mature Christian, and for the one who reads for both pleasure and profit, this book is a must." The Harvester